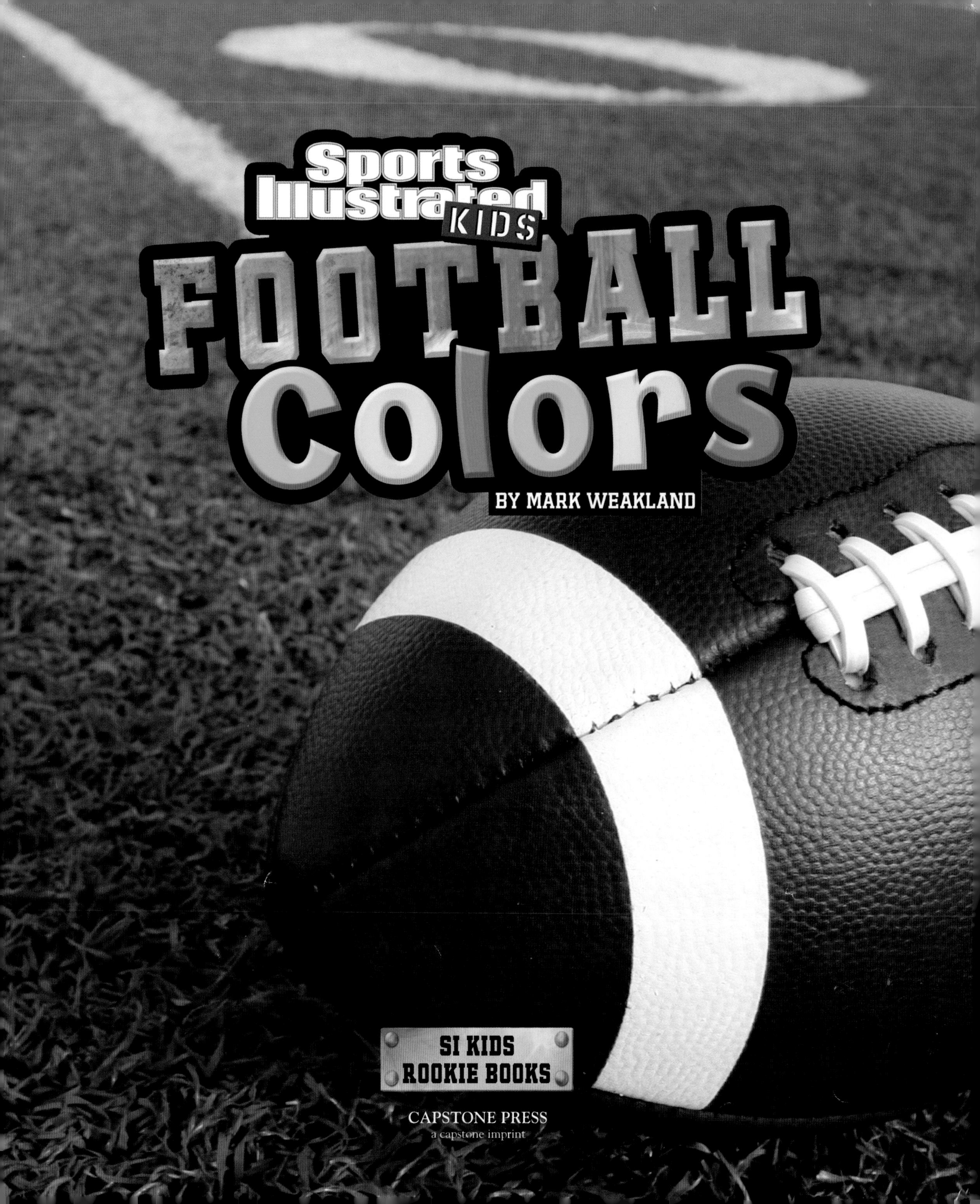

Sports Illustrated KIDS

FOOTBALL Colors

BY MARK WEAKLAND

SI KIDS
ROOKIE BOOKS

CAPSTONE PRESS
a capstone imprint

Sports Illustrated Kids Rookie books are published by Capstone Press,
1710 Roe Crest Drive, North Mankato, Minnesota 56003
www.capstonepub.com

Library of Congress Cataloging-in-Publication Data
Cataloging-in-Publication data is on file with the Library of Congress.
ISBN: 978-1-4296-9959-4 (library binding)

Editorial Credits
Jeni Wittrock, editor; Juliette Peters, designer; Eric Gohl, media researcher;
Eric Manske, production specialist

Photo Credits
Newscom: Cal Sport Media/Max Simbron, 22–23; Shutterstock: David Lee, 1, fstockfoto,
12–13; Sports Illustrated: Al Tielemans, 6–7, 8–9, 26–27, Bob Rosato, 4–5, 20–21, Damian
Strohmeyer, 14–15, 16–17, 18–19, John Biever, cover, 10–11, John W. McDonough, 24–25,
Robert Beck, 2–3, Simon Bruty, 28–29

Printed in the United States of America in North Mankato, Minnesota.
092012   006933CGS13

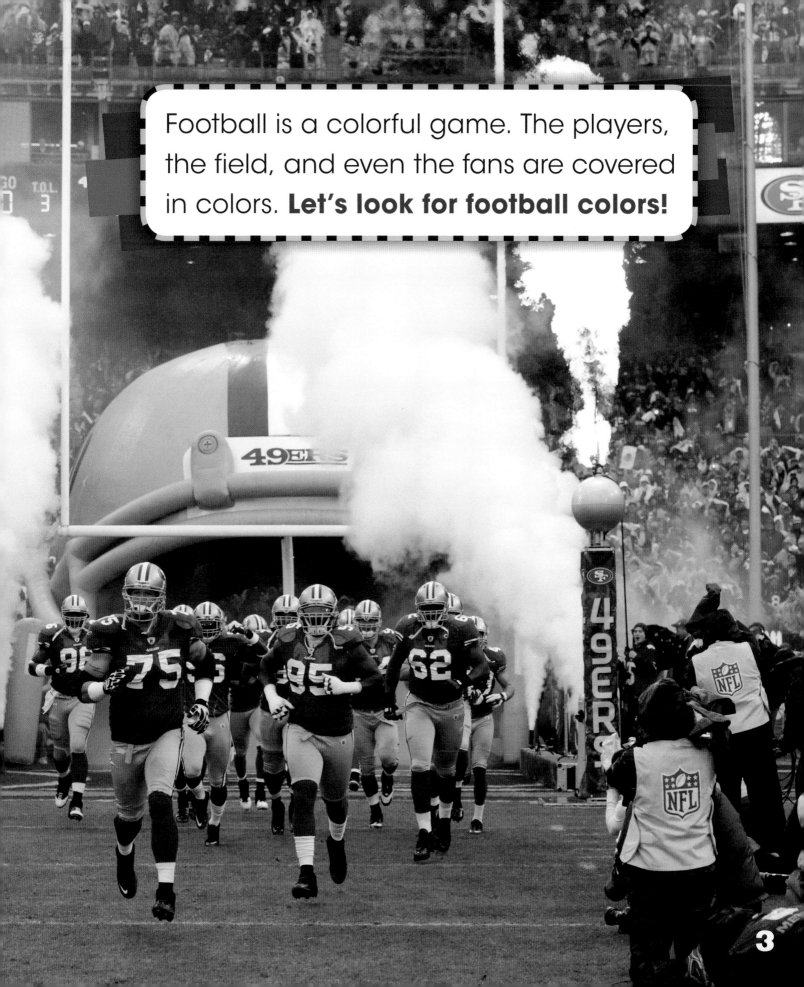

Football is a colorful game. The players, the field, and even the fans are covered in colors. **Let's look for football colors!**

Green

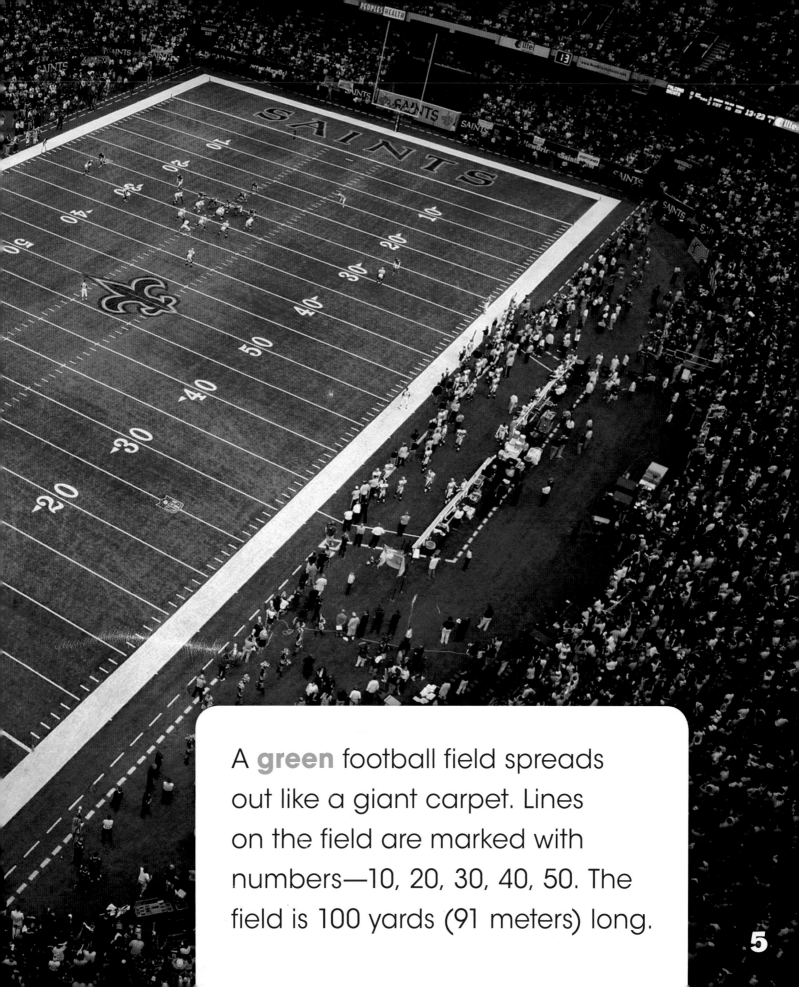

A **green** football field spreads out like a giant carpet. Lines on the field are marked with numbers—10, 20, 30, 40, 50. The field is 100 yards (91 meters) long.

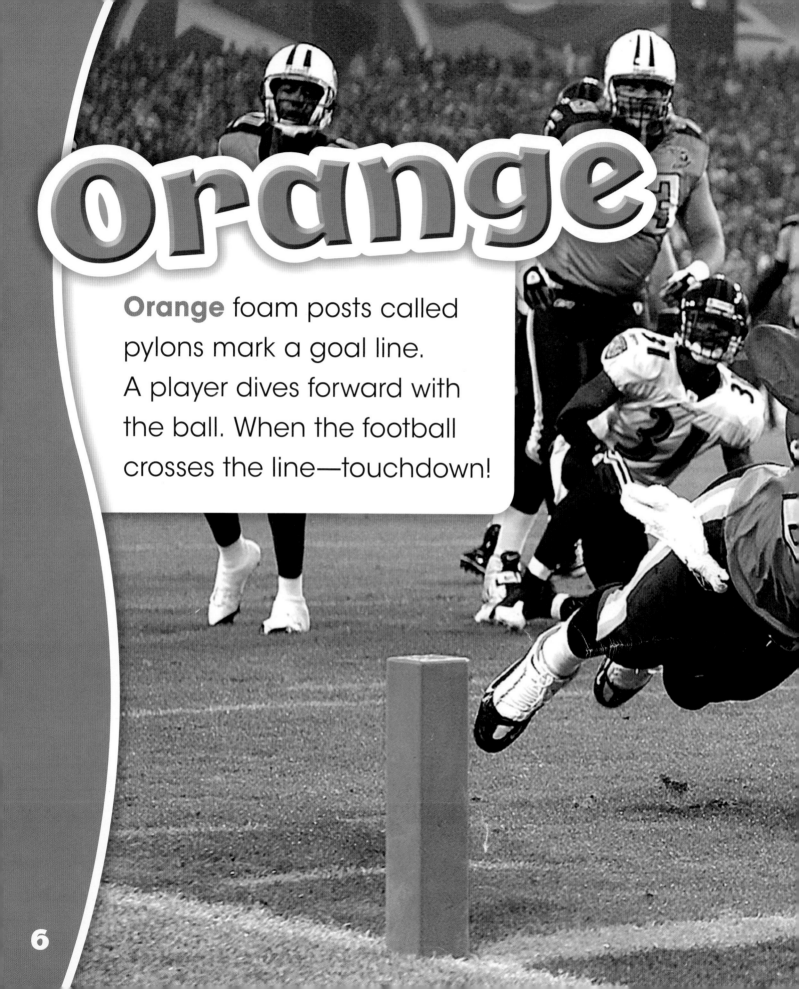

Orange

Orange foam posts called pylons mark a goal line. A player dives forward with the ball. When the football crosses the line—touchdown!

purple

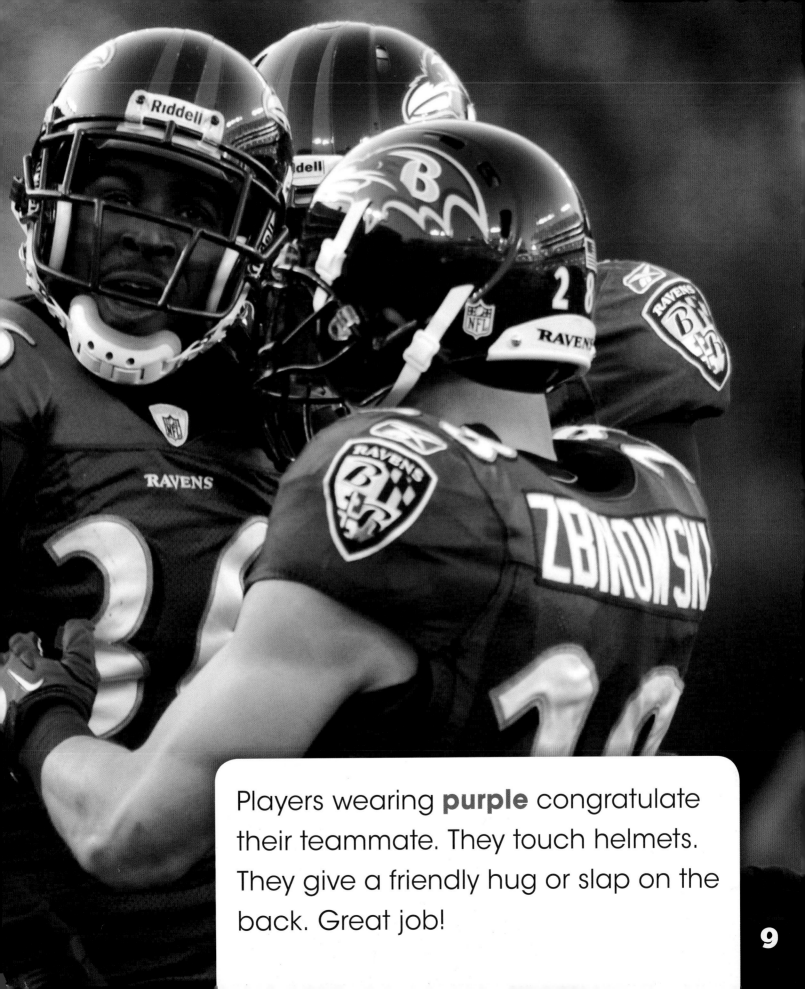

Players wearing **purple** congratulate their teammate. They touch helmets. They give a friendly hug or slap on the back. Great job!

9

Red

A sea of **red** fills a football stadium. Red is one team's special color. The fans' shirts are red. The scoreboard is red. What else is red?

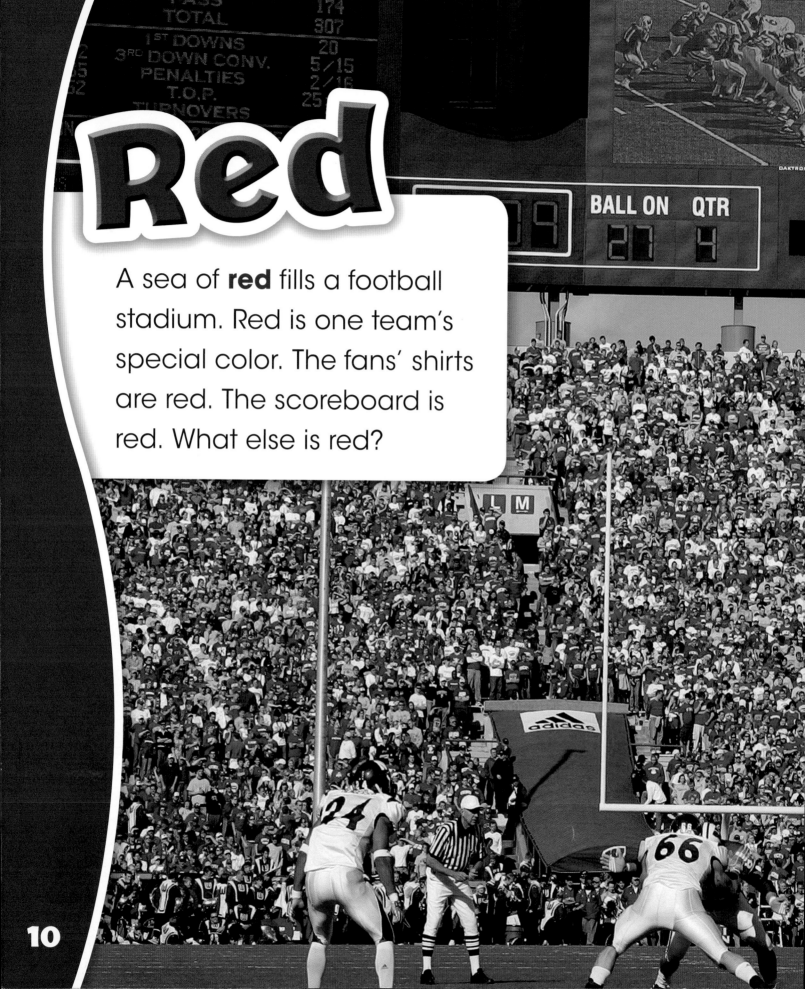

BALL ON   QTR

11

Yellow

A referee throws a **yellow** flag. The flag shows that someone broke the rules. The team may lose yards or a down.

Blue

A goalpost stretches below the bright **blue** sky. A quarterback launches a pass down the field. It's a perfect day for playing football.

Pink

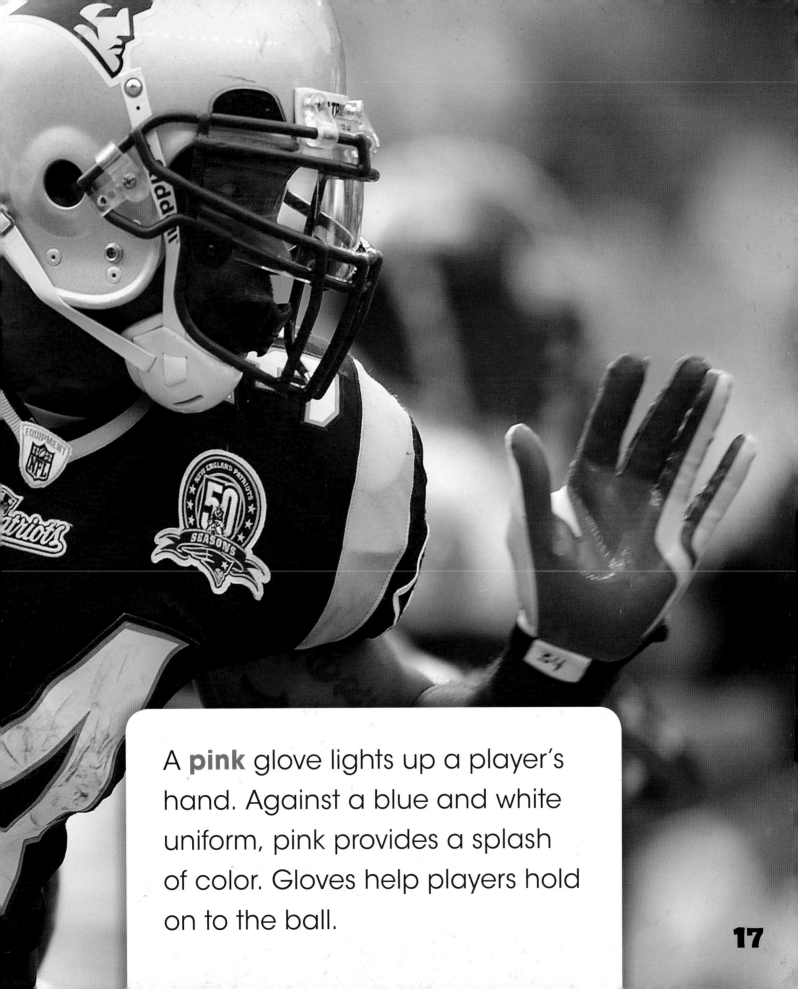

A **pink** glove lights up a player's hand. Against a blue and white uniform, pink provides a splash of color. Gloves help players hold on to the ball.

white

Football is played in the fall and winter. During a snowstorm, a green field soon turns **white**. Players have to be tough to play in the cold, slippery snow.

Brown

Football is played even when it rains. On a wet field, players churn grass and dirt into **brown** mud. The mud covers uniforms, socks, and shoes.

21

Black

Some teams dress in **black**. Black pants cover the players' legs. Black cleats grip the field. Black gloves protect the players' hands.

Rainbow

The crowd cheers! Thousands of football fans come to see their favorite teams play. They dress in a **rainbow** of colors. Red, blue, yellow—what other colors do you see?

25

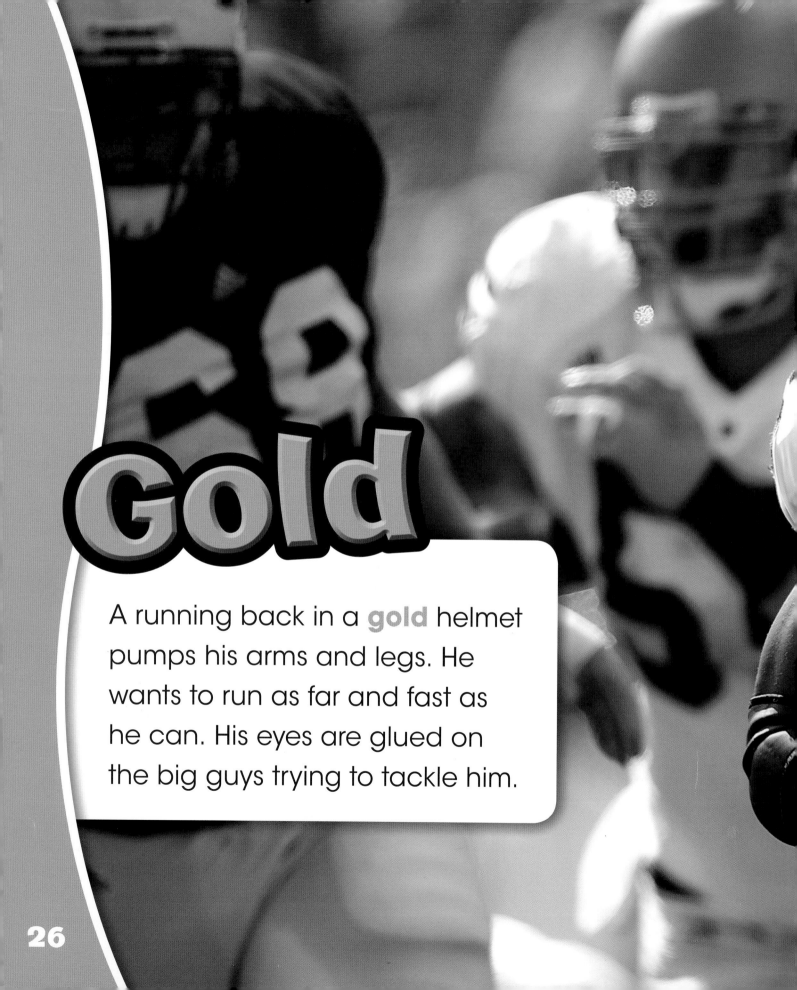

Gold

A running back in a **gold** helmet pumps his arms and legs. He wants to run as far and fast as he can. His eyes are glued on the big guys trying to tackle him.

Red, white,

and Blue

Americans love football!
A giant flag, **red**, white,
and **blue**, covers the field.
Its stars and stripes show off
the colors of the United States.

Glossary

churn—to move roughly

cleat—a shoe with small tips on the bottom to help football players stop or turn quickly

down—a play in football; a team gets four downs to move the football forward 10 yards

goalpost—a post that marks each end of the field; players get points for kicking the ball through the goalposts

protect—to keep safe

pylon—a soft orange post that marks the goal line

scoreboard—a large sign that shows the score, the quarter, and other information about the game

stadium—a large building in which sports events are held

tackle—to stop another player by knocking him to the ground

touchdown—a six-point score in football

Read More

Durrie, Karen. *Football.* Let's Play. New York: AV2 by Weigl, 2011.

Schuette, Sarah L. *Football Frenzy: A Spot-It Challenge.* Spot It. North Mankato, Minn.: Capstone Press, 2013.

Wyatt, James. *Football.* On the Team. New York: Gareth Stevens Pub., 2012.

Internet Sites

FactHound offers a safe, fun way to find Internet sites related to this book. All of the sites on FactHound have been researched by our staff.

Here's all you do:

Visit *www.facthound.com*

Type in this code: 9781429699594

 Check out projects, games and lots more at **www.capstonekids.com**

Index